Golf...is it only a game?

*To my darling wife Wilnelia who could be such a
good golfer if she ever really has the time,
and to J.J. who has the time and I hope will
have the dedication.*

Golf...is it only a game?

Words by Bruce Forsyth

Photographs by Lawrence Levy

SACKVILLE
BOOKS

First published in 1989
by Sackville Books Ltd
Hales Barn, Stradbroke
Suffolk IP21 5JG

© Bruce Forsyth Enterprises and Sackville Books Ltd
Photographs © Lawrence Levy Yours in Sport

Designed and produced by Sackville Design Group Ltd
Art director: Al Rockall
Editor: Heather Thomas
Photography: Lawrence Levy
Photo stylist and co-ordinator: Danielle Fluer
Production: Ruth Nicolas

British Library Cataloguing in Publication Data
Forsyth, Bruce
　Bruce For(e)syth: golf – is it only a game?
　1. Golf
　I. Title
　796.352

　ISBN 0-948615-29-X

Typeset in Sabon by Eta Services Ltd, Beccles, Suffolk
Colour reproduction by Hilo, Colchester, Essex

Printed and bound in Italy by New Interlitho S.P.A., Milan

Contents

When playing golf, or talking about golf, how many times have you seen people shrug their shoulders and say, 'It's *only* a game' when they are really asking themselves, '*Is* it only a game?'

Here's what also it can be: an Obsession, a Religion, a Way Of Life, a Character Builder, a Mental Torture, a Business Lever, a Business Breaker, a Marriage Maker (if they both play), a Home Wrecker (if they don't), a Relaxation (to only a few), a Drug, a Time Taker, a Humbling Experience, a Humiliating Experience, a Walk into The Sunset . . . . . . or a Walk Into Oblivion!

There are probably a few more but I'm sure that you'll have recognised already at least one or two and, if they are mostly on the 'down' side, just stand on the 18th green of your home club and watch the faces of the golfers when it's all over. How many of them look really *happy* about the last few hours they've spent playing their favourite game?

But then again, golf can be fun. If you have the right four-ball and the right sense of humour, the dialogue and ad-lib lines are often worthy of the finest comedy play. Yes, it can be fun!

There are many reasons for taking up the game and mine was a challenge that was to change my way of life. I was in Dundee for Christmas – by the way, never go to Dundee for Christmas, New Year's Eve *yes*, but not Christmas. My partner at the time, Les Roy, and I were playing in a show there for two weeks. We had good digs but our landlord didn't like the way we used to lie in every morning. For a young man (as I was at the time), he thought it was a terrible waste of youth. He said we ought to be out playing golf; we said it was an old man's game!

Anyway, one night after the show, we had a couple of drinks, went back to the 'digs' for supper and the landlord asked us at what time we would like breakfast. We said about 11 to 11.30 and he started on about golf again, telling us that's what we should be doing in the mornings. He went on and on, and, in the end, just to shut him up, we agreed to play the next day.

He woke us up at 7am, which to us was the middle of the night, and no Sergeant-Major could have done a better job of getting us up. He took us to Carnoustie and on the way there explained that, as it was a wee bit frostie, we would play with red balls. He also told us that he would give us two shots on every hole and he would play our best ball. My partner and I gave each other a look of complete confidence.

You will not be surprised to learn, we didn't win one hole and we finished absolutely exhausted. From that day on, I've never believed it's an old man's game.

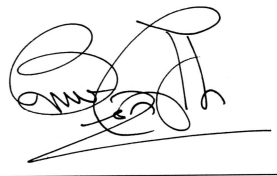

I love playing golf in America, but
it is mostly 'buggy' golf and sometimes
it can be like the start of a Grand Prix.
But from then on 5-hour rounds are very
common. We're much quicker walking!

Always consult your caddy before every shot

Bruce Forsyth: 'I think it's a 5 iron.'

ss Abbot: 'Oh no. Take a 6.'

Bruce: 'But the pin's at the back of the green.'

Russ: 'Yes, sir. But take a 6.'

Bruce: 'But the wind's dead against.'

ss: 'No, sir. It's across.'

13

Bruce: 'Are you sure?'

Bruce: 'I really nailed that one.'

Russ: 'Ooh!'

Russ: 'Ooh! Ooh!'

Russ: 'Ooooooh!'

Russ; 'Ooooooh!' oooooooooooh!' oooooooooooooh!' ooooooooooooooh!'

Some people would do anything to meet Arnold Palmer . . .

Arnold Palmer and I have a lot
in common. We share the
same caddy and we both have
a wife called Winnie.

This Apollo Test Centre is an incredible machine that
can tell you everything about your swing from the take away
right through the ball to your club head speed. I had 48 goes
on it and all the computer kept coming up with was 'No comment!'

Luckily Bob Torrance was there and
he checked my grip.
He noticed that my thumb was going
too straight down the grip.

He suggested that I should move it over
a little to the right.

And he was right. Thank you, Bob!

You've probably seen the Mizuno travelling workshop which follows the European Tour. All the adjustments and alterations to clubs can be done here under the supervision of Barry Willett and his team.

As I wasn't getting much distance, I took my driver along for them to check it. To my surprise, they said that it was perfect, so I asked what could be done. This is where a Japanese gentleman stepped forward, placed my arm in the vice, raised his arm and shouted something in Japanese.

The next thing I remember was waking up in the First Aid Tent. Whatever he did, it worked, and I'm now hitting my driver 220 yards. The only drawback is that I'm hitting my wedge 220 yards as well!

Tip from the Pro: Seve Ballesteros

Playing with Seve Ballesteros in *Pro-Celebrity Golf*
one year, I found my ball lying right against a
steep wall of grass. As far as I was concerned I had
to have a drop – counting a penalty shot – but Seve said,
'No, just hit it with the toe of the club', and,
of course, he was right. So, if you find yourself up
against a wall or a fence or a tree and you have a
line to the green or fairway, just hit it with the toe! Really,
when you think about it, it's just common sense.

There's nothing like a friendly 2-ball . . .

Kenny Lynch:
'Is that a gimme?'

Kenny: 'I said,
is that a gimme?'

Bruce Forsyth:
Yes, Kenny Lynch
always carries
13 clubs in his
bag and his gimme!

Henry Cooper doesn't use a 'gimme' but never ask him for extra shots!

Sartorial elegance

When I played with Rodger Davis on TV, I asked him whether he was wearing socks under his waterproofs. He said, 'Of course I am, Bruce.' I said, 'Isn't that funny? So am I.'

34

Don't let Britain down by going on the golf course like this!   We've all seen 'em!

Sponsorship has become essential to
the modern golfer, but there are those
who get some and those who don't . . . I am available.

Golfwear of the Future

In the worst of weather, the Golfer of the Future could look like this! I bought this thing in Florida and it is really intended to go over the top of the golf bag to keep the clubs dry – but I couldn't help thinking what a wonderful head protector it could be if you were at Turnberry or Pebble Beach, lashed by rain and with a Force 5 gale blowing.

It has so much to offer: good visibility, all-round protection against the elements and no chance of water running down the back of your neck. The only drawback I found was the tendency on the follow through for it to fly off your head. But with a couple of press-studs in the back of your waterproofs it would be stabilized and you could enjoy a dry shot to the full. Extras could include windscreen wipers, central heating, a humidifier, personal stereo etc.

Tip from the Pro: Lee Trevino

One of the best tips on BBC's *Pro-Celebrity Golf* was from Lee Trevino to Sean Connery. The ball was below his feet, needing a chip of about 40 to 50 yards. After Sean had played, Lee showed him that he should have played it with a

closed face which would have helped him to keep the
ball on the left as the ground was running left
to right up to the green. Also, sit back on the
heels a bit. Try it . . . it works. A good shot
to have in your bag.

Why don't they make sand irons like this? Apart from
the grip (which must have the hands apart) everything else
is the same: open stance, aim 4 inches behind the ball, follow right
through and take *plenty* of sand! A guarantee to get out in one.

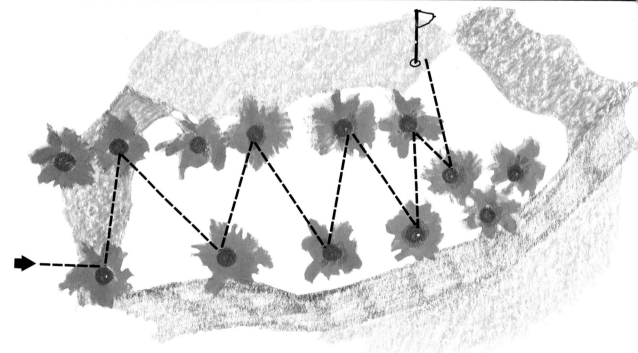

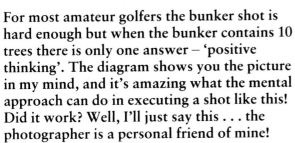

For most amateur golfers the bunker shot is hard enough but when the bunker contains 10 trees there is only one answer – 'positive thinking'. The diagram shows you the picture in my mind, and it's amazing what the mental approach can do in executing a shot like this! Did it work? Well, I'll just say this . . . the photographer is a personal friend of mine!

Spot the odd man out: Tony Jacklin; Sandy Lyle; Bruce Forsyth; Nick Faldo.
(answer on page 122)

46

Junior golf

Most people go to Disney World for the rides and spectacle but I wanted to sample one of the 3 golf courses. So I phoned the pro and asked if Mickey Mouse would like to play a few holes. He said, 'I'm sure he would. He's always wanted to try!' When I arrived, he was just finishing a cheese sandwich that Minnie makes for him every morning as part of his mouse diet. He had a beautiful new set of clubs and head covers that the pro had given him to try. He said he'd like me to try them as well.

On the 1st tee I told him not to be nervous but to relax and just watch me, which he did. I hit my

tee shot and kept my head down. When I looked up,
Mickey was pointing to a bunker in front of the green.

The Walt Disney Company 1989

Now it was his turn, so I gave him a few of
the tips that I had picked up from the pros. I told
him once more not to be nervous and to try to relax,
and he certainly did – his tee shot finished 2 feet from the stick.

Yes, he was a *natural* and a brilliant putter. But, of course,
all mice know how to get into a little hole – it's second nature.

The Walt Disney Company 1989

We played 9 holes and he beat me 3 up with 2 to play.
I do hope he doesn't turn into a *hustler*!

Junior golf

J.J.: 'I bet my daddy can beat *your* daddy.'

Nathalie: 'I bet *my* daddy *can* beat your daddy.'

J.J.: 'Who is your daddy?'

Nathalie: 'Nick Faldo.'   **J.J.:** 'I bet your daddy can beat my daddy too!'

I think that every amateur will agree that the pros play a different game to us. So it's nice to be able to relax and play a game where one is on equal terms. Here I am with Michael King doing just that!

Michael is known to his fellow pros as 'Queenie'.

Tip from the Pro: Lee Trevino

Another good tip from Lee Trevino for bunker play, which I saw him demonstrate on American television, was this: hold the club in the left hand, then open the face of the blade before you place your right hand on the grip. This ensures that you keep the blade open through the swing. If you use your usual grip and then open the face, sometimes there will be a tendency to shut it coming into the sand. But then it's common sense again, isn't it?

At Lake Nona Golf Club, apart from being one of the most
wonderful golf complexes in the world, they also have an
enormous practice ground, which I was using one day when this fella
came up to me. He was wearing a bigger hat than
mine so I thought I'd better listen to him.

First of all, he got me doing this exercise with the club
running across the back of my shoulders to help
get the right pivot.

And then, as you can see from the photographs, he tried to improv

64

He spent about 15 or 20 minutes with me and by the time he left I was hitting the ball really well.

I said, 'Thanks, mate.'
He said, 'The name's David Leadbetter.'
Well, I felt such a fool, especially when I saw
Nick Price, David Frost and Nick Faldo waiting
for their lessons!

Lake Nona is the headquarters of the David Leadbetter Golf School.

The show-off

Stepping on to the tee and playing the first shot of the
day I'm sure is just as hard for the pro as it is for
the amateur. But the difference is that the amateur can be funny . . .

The slogger . . .

. . . and usually a slicer

The short-sighted golfer

The old man

Dial a pro . . .

One of those moments of decision – shall I take a penalty shot or not? Alternatively, as they say on American TV: 'Always consult your local pro'. And that's why I always have my portable telephone with me with a hot line straight to Bernard Gallagher.

Bruce: 'Hello, Bernie.'

Bernie: 'Where are you today, Bruce?'

Bruce: 'Well, I can't take a normal stance. I've got bushes all round the back of the ball, and a tree stopping a normal swing. What should I do?'

Bernie: 'Well there's only one shot you can play by the sound of it. Are you insured against self-inflicted injury?'

Bruce: 'I don't know but what's the shot?'

Bernie: 'Turn your back in the direction of the hole. Grip the club like a croquet mallet, make sure the club face is square behind the ball and hit it between your legs . . . good luck!'

How did I finish in a place like this? There's no shot on – the line is right through that huge log. Mind you, it's not attached to anything, and not

something that's growing. I suppose that it could be
a loose impediment. Let's see how heavy it is – easy.
Sometimes things are not as hard as they seem. I can still get a 5.

When in doubt, always ask for a ruling. PGA officials
John Paramor and Michael Haarer helped me with this one.

Michael: 'Pity this isn't a tee shot.' **John:** 'Yes, he could have driven it away !'

Ode to a lost ball

They seek it here, they seek it there,
Those golfers seek it everywhere.
Is it in heather, is it in hell,
That damned elusive pinnacle.

(With apologies to Dunlop, Slazenger, Spalding, Topflite and Ultra but they just didn't rhyme.)

'Elementary, my dear Watson.'

Whenever I play with Seve, he strongly advocates the power of positive thinking. Here I am trying to put this into practice . . .

Sandy Lyle, US Masters Champion 1988

I often play a game with Sandy as we are both members of Wentworth. But the only trouble is that after every 3 or 4 holes you have to keep stopping to massage his feet.

Nick Faldo, US Masters Champion 1989

I read in a magazine that Nick Faldo always cuts and files his nails down just before every tournament. This is strange because when I'm going to do a show where I play the piano I do the same thing. The fingers feel more sensitive and I suppose the day could come when there is a manicurist stationed at the 1st tee! (I must find out if there is a medical reason for this.)

An important part of any big tournament is the courtesy cars and the girls who drive them. Peter Alliss often needs a car in a hurry but on this occasion he might have preferred to have waited a little longer . . . I really enjoyed playing this joke on my old Pisces pal.

Top picture left: I'm fifth from the right.

I love tree-lined courses but how many times
have you faced this situation?
When you've summed it up, why play a cut shot
round it if you can cut right through it?

We can always learn from pros
like Mark McNulty – but never interrupt
them when they're in the office.

Tip from the Pro: Jerry Pate

Another year, I was playing with Jerry Pate. My ball was behind a bush, so I told him I was just going to chip back on the fairway. He said, 'Hold on a minute, Bruce. Let's have a look. The bush isn't very thick. What club would you normally take from this distance?' I replied that I would probably use a wedge. He said, 'OK. Hit a 9 iron right through it.' I said, 'What?' 'Just hit a normal shot and it will go through.' Well, you can imagine how I felt, and on TV as well. But I hit the shot with good contact and the ball went right through the bush onto the green! And I've got it on tape! The bush must not be too thick, but if you get the chance, try it.

At the 1989 Dunhill Masters Pro-Am at Woburn, I had the pleasure of playing with Ian Woosnam. One of our other partners was Siobhan Keogh who played off 1.

Siobhan wasn't allowed to come in here with us, but people do wonder what goes on in the locker room after the game . . .

DUNHILL BRITISH MASTERS

LOCKER ROOM

PLAYERS ONLY

VISITO LOCKER

. . . I'm sure that part of Ian Woosnam's power is from the forearms. This form of wrestling is very popular and much easier than I thought!

We asked some golfers and celebrities to comment on Bruce's swing. Here are their comments:

Brian Barnes
'With a swing like this he'll always make a good dancer.'

Tony Jacklin
'The top of the backswing is not too bad, the head moves very quickly. Not one of my three choices for a Ryder Cup team spot.'

John Robertson (Publisher of *Golf World* magazine)
'With a swing like that, give it 20 years and he'll make our instruction panel.'

Ian Woosnam
'Nice swing. If his chin wasn't so big he'd be able to get the club a little more upright . . . Not bad considering he's off 12 . . . 14? He does well.'

Bruce Forsyth
Actually, my handicap is 11 in England, and 10 in Spain. They can say what they like, but in the past year I've played the best golf of my life – or rather in my 40 golfing years. So never think that as you get older you can't get better . . . *you can!*

106

Golf's a wonderful game . . . even a tiddler like me can play with the Great White Shark.

The extra long putter is becoming very popular
in the United States, especially on the senior tour.
Sam Torrance is one of the first in Europe to be
seen using it and I must say, after watching him
putt and talking to him about this method, he really
does have a great deal of faith in it. However, he
did say that he wished he had a chin like mine
giving him a better anchor for the pendulum swing!

This is where they all differ . . . putting

▲ I was lucky to be in the winning team at the 1989 Volvo Pro-Am at Wentworth, and here I am getting a putting lesson from our team captain, Howard Clark. As you can see, with his method you just can't miss! Even Howard couldn't believe his eyes.

A similar method is used by Tommy Nakajima, ▶ the Japanese golfer. He gets his caddy, or in my case a semi-friend (Karim), to line a club across his knees parallel to the hole. Just take the club back and then forward on that line.

Somebody gave me this putter.

Bernhard Langer wanted to buy it but I couldn't
sell it to him – I use it to clear the drains!

Some embarrassing moments

I played with Telly Savalas in the Charity Golf Tournament at the R.A.C. Golf Club a few years ago. Now I always thought that it was a gimmick that Kojak was always licking a lollipop. But to my amazement, halfway through the round, he looked in his golf bag and pulled out a lollipop which he then unwrapped and stuck in his mouth. Then he selected his club and, still with the lollipop in his mouth, played his shot which turned out to be a wicked slice. He mumbled something and then I said to him, 'It's your own fault, Telly, that's where the lollipop was pointing!'

My most embarrassing golf moment was at Finchley Golf Club, playing with Brian Barnes. There had been a lot of rain so the ground was very soft. I had to play off a sloping fairway but I still thought I could play a 3 wood. The ball was below my feet; I took my stance and made my swing which felt quite good. I looked down the fairway and then Brian shouted, 'It's still there'. I shouted back 'Where?', looking where the ball had been as there was no sign of it. On further investigation, it had gone straight into the ground and somehow, with it being so wet and soggy, the grass had sucked it in and covered the top of it.

Of other embarrassing moments, my wife Wilnelia has accounted for two, both naturally before she knew anything about the game. The first time was in Florida, when I asked her to ride in a buggy with me so that she could see what golf was all about. Now in Puerto Rico, where she comes from, baseball is the game of the island. I wasn't playing all that well and I was just about to hit my shot when I heard, 'Come on, Brucie Baby!'. Well, I wish a camera had been on me; I would love a keepsake of the look I gave her.

The second time was in Spain. I was playing in a competition and I couldn't find the ball in the rough. Quite a few people were helping including my darling Winnie. All of a sudden I heard her shout, 'I've found it'. I was so thrilled until I turned round and saw her holding it in her hand, waving it above her head with that wonderful smile she has! A two shot penalty.

If you can sink an important putt on the last green, it can make your day.

What a shame there was nobody there!

Holes-in-one!

I have had two holes-in-one (to date). The first one was at White Webbs Golf Course, Enfield. *I was on my own!* It was the 7th, a short hole of 180 yards, slightly downhill. The visibility was not good; I suppose you could only see clearly for about 100 yards. I played the shot, it felt good and I walked towards the green. As I got closer, I couldn't see the ball on the green and I couldn't understand this because it did feel a good shot. I walked closer still and then noticed a little bump up against the flag stick and of course it turned out to be the ball. I've told many audiences this and they never believe me. But I can assure you it is absolutely true and if any of you have had a similar experience, you have my sympathy!

My second hole-in-one is better documented – it was on 26th April 1979 at The Las Vegas Country Club. I was playing with Bob Newhart (the wonderful American comedian), Jack Jones (the sensational singer), Anthony Newley's drummer and a croupier whose name escapes me. Bob, who is a very good golfer, hit the first shot with a 6 iron and it was a good one, about 8 feet from the stick. I played next with a 5 iron and it did feel special. It just took one bounce and rolled about 6 feet right into the hole! Well, we all went mad, especially Jack Jones, who always seems so 'laid back'. He jumped so high in the air that his voice nearly went up an octave!

That is not the end of the story. The Las Vegas Country Club is one of the many clubs in the United States that does not allow money to be handed over the counter at the bar – you have to be a member and put it on your account – so, try as hard as I did, I couldn't buy anyone a drink!

We got drunk all the same but at poor Bob Newhart's expense making it a very cheap hole-in-one for me! The club also gave me some great momentos including the plaque in the photograph with the ball I used mounted in front of a picture of the hole. It was a lovely touch and it would be nice if clubs over here did something similar.

Most men hate shopping . . . unless it's in the pro shop.
Then we go mad!

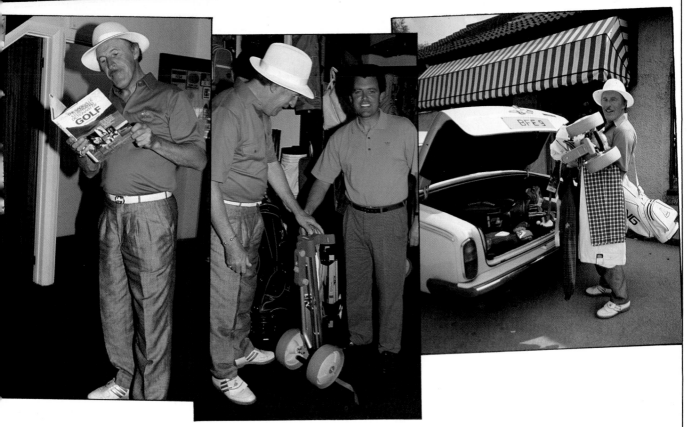

I always like to play a few holes with my wife
Wilnelia, and sometimes, if we find a nice bunker,
we stay there for the rest of the day . . . or
until the tide comes in.

Always sign your card immediately.

'No, son. I'm not Seve Ballesteros.'

Bruce's tip

Now here's a tip from me. Have you ever had the ball
stop on the edge of the green right up against the
fringe, making it impossible to ground your putter
properly? Of course, you have. Well, I've found that if you
place the putter 4 to 5 inches behind the ball, use quite a long
backswing and go right through to the hole, it's quite a good
method. In fact, I've holed a few from that sort of lie.

Answer to Spot the odd man out:
Bruce Forsyth – the other three can't tap dance.

Gambling on the course

**Maybe the best tip of all . . . as Jimmy Tarbuck says,
'Never play for more money than you can afford!'**

123

The St Andrews Lament

The wind did blow,
  ye could hear the snow

As the ball hit the bairn
  in the burn.

But he didn'a wilt
  with a ball up his kilt

In a place
  there was nae return.

(by Lynch and Forsyth with apologies to Robbie Burns)

BRUCE ● FORSYTH

10th May, 1989

Jack Nicklaus Esq.

Dear Jack,

I've had the pleasure of playing with many, many famous golfers including:

Bernhard Langer
Seve Ballesteros
Greg Norman
Nick Faldo
Gary Player
Peter Alliss
Harold Henning
Mark O'Meara
Johnny Miller
Ben Crenshaw
Ray Floyd
Rodger Davis

Lee Trevino
Sandy Lyle
Tom Watson
Ian Woosnam
Arnold Palmer
Bobby Locke
Bob Charles
Jerry Pate
Tom Weiskopf
Craig Stadler
Tony Jacklin
Mark McNulty

The fact I've never had the honour of walking some fairways with you, and playing beside you, makes my golfing life incomplete.

Should you be in the Wentworth area anytime soon, please come and be my guest for the day.

Yours sincerely,

Bruce Forsyth

P.S. I've just thought of a few more, Jack:

Clive Clark; Michael King; John O'Leary; Mark James; Paul Way; Sam Torrance; David J. Russell; Howard Clark; Christy O'Connor; Bernard Gallacher; Dave Thomas; Brian Barnes; Neil Coles; Jack Newton; Eamonn D'Arcy; Ronan Rafferty; Chi Chi Rodriguez; Doug Sanders; Tommy Horton; John Jacobs; Manuel Pinero; Ian Mosey; Larry Nelson; John Davies; Bruce Critchley; Peter McEvoy; Peter Townsend; David A. Russell; Antonio Garrido; David Feherty; Gordon J. Brand; Max Faulkner; Guy Wolstenholme; Manuel Calero; Jose-Maria Olazabal; Vicente Fernandex; Gordon Brand Jnr; Fuzzy Zoeller; Hugh Baiocchi.

I'm looking forward to meeting Jack. The nearest I've ever come to shaking his hand was when he won the 1986 US Masters.

Jack Nicklaus

May 30, 1989

Dear Bruce:

Thank you for your letter. You know, I've been hearing Greg and Ben and Lee and a lot of the other guys talk about the great experience they had playing golf with Bruce Forsyth. Now, I enjoy a good time just as much as the next guy, and I was beginning to wonder why you never invited me!

Actually, my schedule is usually pretty tight, but if I'm in the Wentworth area, I will do my best to give you a call. I just hope my game is up to yours!

Best regards,

Some of the things we didn't need to use, but our thanks and acknowledgements go to the following people, companies and organisations who helped us in the preparation of this book:

Acknowledgements

Apollo Swing Analyser and Test Vehicle for the European Tour
Bay Hill Golf Club, Orlando, Florida
Bernard Gallagher Pro Shop
Karim Bonakdar
Central Sales and Marketing Ltd [for supplying the Character Golf Club covers)
Corona (for all the cigars that Eric Sykes has put down on a teeing area and Bruce has trodden on)
The courtesy girls from the Volvo Tour
Dunhill British Masters
Fox's Marina Ipswich Ltd
Hallmark Hampers
Jack Hayward (for the old plus-fours used in the Old Man sequence)
International Management Group
Lake Nona Golf Club, Orlando, Florida

The Mizuno Workshop and Barry Willett (consultant to the Mizuno Company)
The PGA European Tour
'POWA' Caddy (for helping Bruce recharge his batteries)
Pro-Quip (for keeping Bruce dry and warm . . . in Florida!)
James Sunley
Volvo Cars
The Walt Disney Company
Wentworth Golf Club and officials
Ian Wilson (especially between 10am and 1pm)
Woburn Golf Club
Yours in Sport

And our thanks to all the celebrities and pros who kindly agreed to appear or be quoted in the book including: Russ Abbot, Peter Alliss, Seve Ballesteros, Brian Barnes, Howard Clark, Henry Cooper, Nick and Nathalie Faldo, Michael Haarer, Tony Jacklin, Siobahn Keogh, Michael King, David Leadbetter, Sandy Lyle, Kenny Lynch, Mark McNulty, Jack Nicklaus, Greg Norman, Arnold Palmer, John Paramor, John Robertson, Jimmy Tarbuck, Bob Torrance, Sam Torrance, Tom Watson and Ian Woosnam.

And finally we acknowledge the celebrities and pros whom it was impossible to include because of their commitments, especially Ronnie Corbett for willing to be included in this book but who was unfortunately in France. We wanted him to try Sam Torrance's putter!